COLOUR PHOTOGRAPHY

Hans Sponholz

CW00550015

SPECTRUM
Colour Books

FOULIS

A SPECTRUM COLOUR BOOK

COLOUR PHOTOGRAPHY · HOW TO GET THE BEST RESULTS FROM YOUR CAMERA AND FILMS is published by G T Foulis & Co Ltd of Sparkford, Yeovil, Somerset BA22 7JJ England.
First published in German under the title **FARBFOTOGRAPHIE** by Hallwag AG of Bern, Switzerland

© English language edition, G T Foulis & Co Ltd 1975

ISBN 0 85429 505 4

All rights reserved. No part of this book may be reproduced or transmitted in any form or by any means, electronic or mechanical, including photocopying, recording or by any information retrieval or storage system, without permission in writing from the copyright holders.

English language translation Derek Van Abbe for "Accurate Translations", Maidenhead, Berkshire
Printed and bound by J H Haynes & Co Ltd Sparkford, Yeovil, Somerset
Photos Hans Sponholz and Heinrich Hofmanner
Cover photo Les Brazier (courtesy Tilzey, Yeovil)

CONTENTS

BY WAY OF INTRODUCTION

The world around us is teeming with colour. Our eyes luxuriate in the soothing green of the meadows and the riotous splendour of the flowers. The blue of the skies, and the gay tints of the autumn leaves, all these things are a never-failing source of pleasure. Things become miserable as soon as some swathe of mist comes along to blot out the colours. Can you wonder, then, that amateur photographers are more and more desirous of fixing for good and all this world of ours in its natural colourings? Black-and-white photography as a hobby is being left at the post, despite its continuing right to exist. Recently in one year a total of 174 million films were developed in Europe, 46 million of them were colour slides and 59 million colour negatives; only what were left, over and above these totals were black-and-white: the developing laboratories are being pushed to the limit to keep up with the steadily rising total of colour films. In the labs too you will find men who whisper, to whoever is prepared to listen, of yet another of the howlers being committed all the time by well-intentioned beginners. This book, written by a practising photographer for other practising photographers, is some attempt to cut down the number of miss-shots by eliminating the causes of the mistakes and contributing to the making of better pictures.

COLOUR-FILM AS A MEDIUM

What sort of camera?

If what you want is a simple everyday snap for your family album, you can get by with a camera which will not cost you a lot of money. The only rule here is not to forget the old reminder never to take a picture without having the sun behind you. If there is no sun you can always use an electronic or a magnesium flash. If your aim is something a bit more sophisticated you will keep your eyes open for a pricier camera with colour-corrected lens. The 'colour-lens', as it is frequently called, is not a very marked improvement on the colour-corrected lens.

Should you decide to buy a new camera, you will find yourself faced by a vast range of choice and really in need of expert advice. The amateur ought to go for the smaller format of film then, these coming from the 35mm size of camera. Larger cameras producing a larger format, i.e. 6 x 6cm and 6 x 7cm cameras, are acceptable for colour photography purposes, especially if you are after a picture which will be most suitable for publication in print such as books and magazines.

You may need to consider

Rules-of-thumb and traditional stand-bys which are good enough for black-and-white photography can only be used to a limited extent when making colour shots. Colour film is a totally different medium from black-and-white, even though they come out of similar boxes. This involves psychological considerations as well as technical ones. With practice and experience it is not all that difficult to get round the technical problems, but the psychological hang-ups are horses of a different colour. You need to think very deeply when you come up against the question, "Is this worth a colour shot?" It depends in the end on the nature of the subject. A green field with red poppies will look like nothing on earth in black-and-white; it won't look its best unless in colour. Not that I am implying that black-and-white is finished for good now. The two media can carry on quite happily side by side, like drawing compared with oil-painting. Some subjects look more urgent and convincing in black-and-white than colour. If it is

5

the colour that makes your picture, use colour film; if it is an outstanding shape you're after, use black-and-white. There are no other golden rules.

How to use natural and artificial lighting

Amateurs usually call reversal colour film 'slides', which is a good working simplification. It is fair enough to do this, because the main use of reversal colour film is to provide slides suitable for projecting. Reversal-colour film is made up of three layers which are sensitised, each in a special way, to blue, green or red. The emulsions from which they are made incorporate elements of the corresponding complementary colours, yellow, purple and greenish-blue. The film is coated overall with a special protective coat. Reversal-colour film comes in two specific types, daylight film (for **natural lighting**) and film specially treated for **artificial lighting**. The former is adapted to an average 5500°, the latter to (calculated or ca.) 3000 Kelvin. For further details see page 15. Film for natural lighting is marked with the letter N, film for artificial lighting with the letter A. The letter C preceding denotes colour-film. Note the following:

	Agfa	Kodak
Reversal-colour film for natural light	CN	. . .chrome
Reversal-colour film for artificial light	CA	. . .chrome, type B
Colour-negative film for both natural and artificial light	CNA	. . .colour

Experienced amateurs will find no difficulty in 'adapting' film for natural and artificial lighting by means of filters, but are advised to employ the grade of film which is specifically designed for the variety of lighting which is to be used. Thus natural-lighting film may be adapted to artificial-lighting by the interposition of a -series blue filter and artificial-lighting film adapted to natural-lighting by the interposition of a -series red-brown filter. Since the results will not always turn out as you intended, do try to keep natural-lighting film for daylight, and artificial-lighting film tor artificial light. There are exceptions to every rule and there may be circumstances in which you may well need to use not artificial lighting but daylight film for twilight or street-lighting conditions.

You have not got much leeway!

When you are using black-and-white film it does not make much odds if - within limits, of course - you do occasionally over- or under-expose the subject. Such slight divergencies can be ironed out by care in developing and by choosing an appropriate grain of paper. This is not so when using reversal-colour film. In this sort of picture over-exposure gives you faded and washed-out colours, and under-exposure makes the film very dark and nearly opaque. This is almost the direct reverse of what you notice when you are using black-and-white film. And that is not all: faulty lighting will give you transposed colouring and maybe precisely the colours you didn't want. The great advantage of reversal-colour film is that it gives you a translucent image with accurate colouring, a real diapositive slide which has, when projected, a quite astonishing ability to give off radiance, of a sort which no coloured illustration can begin to compete with. You can make coloured illustrations from the slide, but these will only fail to be satisfactory if you've got contrasts, which are too strong. You can also make a negative from it and end up with a perfectly normal black-and-white picture. Slides can be copied an indefinite number of times.

Colour-negative film

As the title indicates, on development colour-negative film produces a negative. As in black-and-white photography, bright objects appear dark on the negative, and vice versa. What is more, colours are 'turned inside out' as well. Purple turns to green, yellow comes out as blue, and light green takes the place of dark red. If you combine reversal-colour film with daylight - or artificial-lighting film, colour-negative film may to all intents and purposes be used under any type of lighting, i.e. not only in daylight but under all kinds of artificial light and, of course, when you are using electronic and magnesium flashes. The only thing which does not suit it is a mixture of lighting which employs sources differing widely from one another.

7

Causes less trouble

Colour-negative film does not need such a closely defined spectrum of lighting as reversal-colour film because you can iron out tiny errors when developing. The greatest advantage is that it does produce excellent coloured snaps for your album. From a really sharp picture you can make a slide, and black-and-white enlargements into the bargain. If you have a well-equipped darkroom handy, you can even develop colour-negative films yourself.

What is DIN?

On the manufacturer's instructions in reversal-colour film you will see the warning, 'Expose according to DIN'. This is supposed to be a helpful hint for you when dealing with subjects under lighting of average brilliance. With reversal-colour the brands all use values between 15 and 23 DIN; with colour-negative the values are between 17 and 21 DIN. It is a well-known experience in black-and-white photography that an increase of 3 DIN means twice the amount of sensitivity. The table appended explains the kinds of applications suited to the two types.

Colour-negative is a very versatile medium, though it has the limitation that slides made from it rarely display the quality we accept as a matter of course with reversal-colour. It is considerably cheaper to buy than reversal-colour, but becomes very dear indeed if you make normal prints from the negatives. It depends on what you want. If you must have slides to show, use reversal-colour; if it is normal prints you are after, go for colour-negative.

Reversal-colour (slides)	Colour-negative (prints)
diapositives (slides), copies of slides, coloured copies and normal enlargements, black-and-white negatives and copies of such negatives, enlargements in black-and-white colour pictures for printing purposes	coloured display-pictures, coloured copies and enlargements of these on paper, coloured diapositives, black-and-white copies and enlargements taken straight from the colour negative, coloured pictures for use as display snaps.

DIN	14	15	16	17	18	19	20	21	22	23	24	25	26
ASA	20	25	32	40	50	64	80	100	125	160	200	250	320

DIN	27	28	29	30
ASA	400	500	640	800

How to use the correct exposure values

I insisted earlier on the necessity to choose the proper exposure when using reversal-colour film. The manufacturers invariably include an exposure table in with their film; this is not simply a sales gimmick but represents the results of years of experience. As an example I shall give the exposure table for **Agfa Reversal-colour CT18** (shutter speed **1/125th** or **1/100th** sec.). Stop down as for DIN 18 = ASA 50.

Bright sunlight		Shutter 8-11 Stop 13-14
Sun obscured, haze		Shutter 8 Stop 13
Sunshine, but in shadow		Shutter 4-5.6 Stop 11-18
Overcast		Shutter 4 Stop 11
Rain, very poor light		Shutter 2.8 Stop 10

9

Another popular daylight film, **Kodachrome II,** produced by Kodak. is three DIN less sensitive than the Agfa film (DIN 15 = ASA 25) but has the advantage of being much less coarse-grained. These are the figures given by Kodak:

Exposure time 1/60th or 1/50th sec.

Bright sunlight, on light-coloured sand or snow		Shutter 16
Bright light or hazy sunlight (very well-defined shadows)		Shutter 11
Blurred shadow		Shutter 4
Cloudy but bright (no shadows)		Shutter 5.6
Very overcast		Shutter 4

The figures given by both of these manufacturers are valid for the period between two hours after sunrise until two hours before sunset. In the dull seasons of the year it is advisable, even when using these tables, to step up the shutter by a half or one whole value. It depends entirely on whether you are dealing with bright, medium or dark subjects. If you are dealing with sunlight on snow, glacier ice, etc., stop the shutter down from the given values.

Using the exposure-meter

All the colour-film manufacturers insist on the photographer's using a good exposure-meter, precisely because, reversal-colour film is very dicey with respect to correct exposure. Leaving aside the now obsolescent optical meter, we may distinguish two types of exposure-meter: a) the selenium-cell meter; b) the CdS-resistance meter. The most up-to-date form of CdS-meter is the electronic meter. Its cells react with phenomenal accuracy to the slightest differences between lighting conditions. (It is advisable to take the equipment out of its protective cover when using it). It is sometimes held that selenium-cell meters and CdS meters do not give the same readings as each other on account of their employing different types of colour-sensitivity. But, other things being equal, it is nowadays likely that they will coincide. The selenium meter covers a visual angle of 50-60°, which is roughly what you cover of any subject at normal focal length. The battery-powered CdS exposure-meter covers a normal angle of 30°. It has additional optical fittings which allow you to cut this down considerably, so that measurings are possible to any desired finite degree of accuracy. As against the selenium meter, which is quick to react to alterations in light-intensity, the CdS meter is somewhat slower, especially when alternating between light and dark. Both types are precision tools of considerable utility and each has its independent raison d'etre.

How to measure the subject

When using the exposure-meter in the normal way, you aim the cell from the spot where you have set up your camera and point it straight at the subject. With a normal lens you will obtain the same angle of vision in both cases, and the measurement will be valid for all practical purposes. If the meter takes in more than the lens of your camera, or if the subject has lots of strongly contrasting lights and shadows, it may be advisable to use the close-up method and take the meter up to within 12-18 inches (30-40cm) of the subject and 'aim' directly at the part that interests you most. Be careful to stand in such a position that your shadow does not fall on the subject and confuse the reading. In which part ought you to be most interested? If you are using reversal-colour film, aim at the bright (not necessarily the brightest!) part of the subject. It was precisely the other way round when using black-and-white film. When you are using colour-negative film you should aim at the shadows too.

Rule of thumb:

With reversal-colour film, whether under daylight or artificial-lighting conditions, aim the exposure-meter at the brighter areas; with colour-negative film, take sight on the darker parts of your picture.

How to use the exposure-meter

Most of the more recent CdS exposure-meters as well as those using selenium cells, are also equipped for metering the light. If you use them for this, it is necessary to proceed in the opposite way, i.e., you measure from the subject towards the lens. First, put a filter or mask over the meter-cell, because the direct lighting falling on the cell will be much stronger than the light reflected by the subject. Light-metering is used for macro-pictures, for very contrasty subjects and, preferably, under artificial light. It is essential to test your exposure-meter before using it in earnest. It is a sound investment to shoot off a whole reversal-colour reel for test purposes: under any circumstances this is money well spent. Stick to **one** brand of film and get yourself used to adjusting the readings of your exposure-meter to the DIN mark recommended by the manufacturer, say 18, look out a subject of middling brightness with lighting falling from one side or from an angle of 45°. You can also get good results with back-lighting from the side. After careful measurement of the subject, set the result on your camera. Let us assume that the subject demands a 1/125th sec. stop with shutter at 8. Take your first picture, noting carefully both the shuttering and the stopping used. Then take a second picture, opening the shutter an extra half-value but keeping your camera stopped at 1/125th sec. Carry on, setting the shutter at 5.6 for your third picture. In the end you will obtain three pictures, taken at shutter values you have gradually increased. Unless you noted down these figures, the exercise has no point.

Then carry out a second series of tests, narrowing the shutter down each time by one half-value until you reach 16. Then take a further set of three pictures. When the film comes back from the developing lab, you can then make up your own mind as to which settings gave you the best results. If you find that the 1/125th sec. stopping given by the exposure-meter was satisfactory at shutter 8, you can safely stick to a drill involving the setting of the meter to DIN 18/ASA 50. You might, however, discover that you got the best picture with a shutter-setting somewhere between 8 and 11. In that event you would be wise to set the exposure-meter to DIN 19/ASA 64. If it turns out that the picture you took with a shutter setting between 8 and 5.6 was the most satisfactory, go down from DIN 18 to 17/ASA 50 to 40.

Critical contrast

Imagine you are photographing two flower-boxes. In one of them there are pink geraniums and some yellow calceolarias. The contrast between these two colours is infinitesimal. Since the exposure-meter is designed to notice only a small spectrum of contrast, you can quite safely narrow the shutter by one half-value. The second flower-box contains, in addition to the yellow calceolarias and a few white petunias, mainly dark-blue petunias. You cannot miss the strong contrast between the white and the yellow, on the one hand, and the dark blue, on the other. In this case I should widen the shutter by one half-value - only then will you do justice to the violent contrast.

As against this you should avoid over-violent contrasts in your subject; colour-film is much more limited in its ability to bridge contrasts than black-and-white film. Let me give you an example: a bridal couple is leaving the registry office; she in light pink, he in a darker, duller shade. The sunlight is falling in such a way that the bride's shadow is falling over her husband's suit, making it even darker than it is already. Going by the exposure-meter, the bride calls for 1/250th sec. at shutter 8, the groom for a quarter to half a second. This is altogether too much for colour-film; the terrific contrast is way beyond its powers to overcome. In this case you will do better in black-and-white. Where contrasts are altogether too striking you will get either the bright or the dark colours wrong. The brights will turn out washed out and faded, the darks altogether too rich. It is worth making a note of the rule that colour-film does best through colours and not through violent contrasts of light and dark.

Keep your eyes open for lighting contrasts as well as contrasting colours. Feininger lays it down that the lighting-scale is the difference between the largest and smallest amount of light which is infusing the subject (lights and shadows). The reflection-scale is the difference between the brightest and the darkest coloured parts of a subject lighted uniformly overall. We call the product of these two scales the subject-contrast. Experience teaches that the best results from colour-photography are obtained when the lighting-contrast in subjects giving a middling reflection-scale does not exceed 3:1; in the case of Agfa reversal-colour 4:1; and in the case of Agfa colour-negative not more than 2-3:1. If the contrasts are stronger still, you would be wise to use an electronic or a blue flash, even when photographing in the open, in order to scale down the contrasts.

Rule of thumb

With reversal-colour slight under-exposure is more bearable than over-exposure. Colour-negative is different: slight over-exposure is much more desirable on the whole than keeping the exposure on the mean side.

The dreaded blue interference

The eye always sees a white wall or a patch of snow as white, no matter what time of day it meets it. In actual fact we overlook the phenomenon that the white is changing all the time, according to the sun's height in the sky. At high noon there are bluish tinges in the shadows; and early in the morning and late in the afternoon, the white has a tendency to turn slightly yellow, orange or pink. Around midday it is the shady sides which tend to come out on your colour-film with the dreaded blue interference. This is no general condemnation of blue as a colour, if it is in its proper place, as in the azure Southern skies or as the colour of cornflowers and gentians. But on a coloured photograph this dead blue colour is shocking, as any expert advertising man will tell you. Shops do not tie up parcels in blue; they stick to the warmer colours, yellow, orange, red or light green. Mild blue interference is tolerable on some slides on some occasions, because the luminosity takes the edge off it; but on a contact-print it will not do at all. How does this interference come about? Well, the shady sides of the subject are shielded from the sun and get their light exclusively from the dark-blue sky. If the blue sky is covered with drifting white clouds, these act as reflecting screens. This is the reason why colour-photography experts recommend - and not, as you can imagine, solely for artistic reasons - giving preference to a cloudless sky. As against blue interference, a mild yellow interference, such as you can get with evening sunshine, is bearable and much more pleasant. It is a warm tone and makes you feel more cheerful.

Colour-temperature

Colour-films are prepared for a definite colour-temperature, and this varies according to use. What is colour-temperature? It is a concept borrowed from Physics. Daylight is 5600° Kelvin. The scale begins at the absolute zero point of normal temperature, -273°C. Since an electric-light bulb gives off a reddish rather than a bluish light, and a black object gives off reddish light at 3200° Kelvin, a much lower temperature, films for use in natural light are prepared for a colour-temperature of ca. 5600° Kelvin, and artificial-light film for ca. 3200°. Electronic flashes emit a quasi-sunlight brilliance of between 5500 and 6000° Kelvin; so do blue-tinged flashes. If you use intinted flashes, they give off a yellowish light with a colour-temperature of between 3500 and 4500° Kelvin. Note that colour-temperature is independent of the source employed. Professional photographers, who do a lot of work out-of-doors, use an accurate measuring-gauge to find the colour-temperature, but amateurs do not need it save in exceptional cases. Our modest needs are adequately met by our employing a so-called Skylight filter especially where you are dealing with green reflected light under leafy trees or with blue reflected light in shadow. This softens reflected colours and heightens the warm, without exaggerating either. Filters such as are used in black-and-white photography should not **under any circumstances** be used for colour-photography.

There is no need to alter stopping-time when using the Skylight filter. The colour temperature of natural lighting is, however, not constant, as already noted. The following figures demonstrate its range:

15

Morning and evening sunshine	ca. 3-4000°K
1-2 hours after sunrise and just before sunset	ca. 4-5600°K
Blue, cloudless sky	ca. 4500-7000°K
Blue sky with white clouds	ca. 4300-6000°K
Overcast or grey sky	ca. 6500-10,000°K
Blue sky, shadows on open ground	ca. 7-26,000°K

Where the colour-temperature is high, as in the case of a completely overcast sky, the slide will be matt; where it is much higher, as in the case of a vivid blue sky with shadows on open ground, you are liable to get strong blue interference. Where the colour-temperature is low, as is the case with sunshine early and late, the colours on the slides look particularly warm; where the colour-temperature is very low, as at sunrise and sunset, the slide will probably suffer from yellow or red interference. Do not risk taking pictures in colour between midday and 2 p.m. (or to be on the safe side, 3 p.m.) because those are the hours when there is altogether too much blue coming from the light outside.

Using flashes under natural lighting conditions

I have already suggested that it is a good idea to use electronic or bulb flashes, and blue flashes into the bargain, in order to lighten the dark parts when you are taking photographs in the open air. I will extend this to pictures taken against the light, so long as you are careful not to try, by giving overmuch flash, to get too strong an effect. The best thing is to use the exposure-meter on the subject first, set the camera accordingly and then narrow the shutter by one value. When you are taking a macro-picture you may not be able to dispense with flashes, especially when your picture includes living objects which will not keep still in one place.

SOME USEFUL PRACTICAL HINTS

Compared with black-and-white photography, colour-photography is still more or less in its infancy, despite the great technical progress that has been made since the Second War. No one agrees as yet whether colour-pictures should represent Nature as it is or whether they should improve on it. Painters worry much less: they leave out anything which does not fit their design and they add as much as they please. We will not become involved in that dispute; it is a field in which, for the most part, personal taste is everybody's main criterion. Nevertheless we ought not to gloss over one or two points which are basic. I have already drawn a distinction between 'warm' and 'cold' colours. The great differences between these lead me on to give you some guides to the posing of subjects which may be useful. Colours give the effect of space and depth; there are particular background and foreground and even middle-ground, colours. The foreground colours include notably red, yellow and orange, i.e. the 'warm' colours. Blue is best pushed into the background; it is the 'cold', far-off colour, and is indispensable for hinting at immense distances. The ideal intermediary between 'cold' and 'warm' is green.

Tip:

Build up your composition from the foreground, using red, orange and yellow first, with green and then blue to follow, if you want to emphasise middle and background.

Simplicity and clarity

People who are buying picture postcards usually clamour to get 'as much as possible' on them. Do not try to take colour-pictures of that sort. Your picture has definitely got something to say, but it will be that much more convincing if you have said what it was you wanted to say, simply and clearly. Cramming everything in merely clutters it up. The real expert is the person who discreetly restricts himself to bare essentials. This is the right way to show that your subjective reactions are really worth expressing and able to create an impression. A simple change of viewpoint may open up novel and not yet explored angles. A detail from a big ensemble can be more telling than a vast panoramic view. It is a fortunate photographer who is in the position of being able to substitute a lens with longer focal length say 90-105 or even 135mm for his ordinary one. Concentrate on colours not shapes. It is a good thing to have patches of complementary colours standing up against big splashes of colour, but do not let the complementary colours steal the show. Just imagine you have been climbing up a hill or a tower and are gazing out over a landscape which looks perfect, a panorama of almost inconceivable beauty crying out to be commemorated by your colour-picture. It can, nonetheless, still turn out extremely disappointing: you did not create a proper foreground; you lost all sense of perspective in the general building-up; no one can make out the detail. Foreground is tremendously important; it can be adequate if you highlight a blossoming bud or an autumnal spray of leaves.

Colourful does not mean flashy

Some gardeners trip themselves up by sowing hosts of bulbs without any plan, with the result that in the long run there are lots of tiny blobs of colour, scattered madly all over the place. The amateur photographer can make the same mistake just as easily by trying to cram too much colour into the one print. He wants it to be colourful, but only succeeds in getting a muddle of colours which leaves the viewer wondering whether he is on his

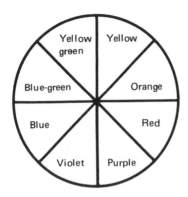

The Colour disc

head or his heels, because there is not a single point of rest for the eye. Your gaze is pulled hither and thither all the time. There must be some sense of order in a picture. You do not have to measure it out with a theodolite, but it must be there all the same. If you have one dominant colour, what is the harm in having little dabs of it elsewhere? The same goes for other complementary colours. If you want to know what complementary colours are, look at the spectrum ring (above). Try looking at an intensely green meadow for a very long time and then shut your eyes: the odds are you will be seeing red!

There is a vertical line in the middle of the spectrum ring which marks off the warm colours (on the right) from the cold (on the left). The colours which are diagonally opposite each other are the 'complementary' colours; those which are side by side are related. There is nothing against employing complementary colours, but do not overload your picture with two equally large patches of colour. This is an error which cannot be denegated loudly enough. If you want **one** dominant colour, all the others will have to put up with playing a modest second fiddle. Never jumble together two or three sets of complementary colours.

Photograph without
Pol-filter

Photograph with
Pol-filter

The polarisation filter

I told you earlier how wise you would be always to use the Skylight filter. This requires no additional exposure-time but cuts down or shuts out ultra-violet light and keeps a tight rein on blue and green interference. The extra filter I am now recommending will set the amateur back a good bit more. This is the polarisation filter, called Pol-filter for short. It does require a 2½ times lengthening of exposure-time, but, when you see everything it does for you, you should not bother too much about taking it in your stride. It strengthens up any sky that is on the pallid side, and highlights the white clouds for you. It strengthens considerably the green fields and sea. It will cut down or do away with reflections, if you do not want them - by that I mean reflections on water, glass, lacquer, paint, polished wood, etc. and wet asphalt, but not metal. This is not the place to dilate on the concept of polarisation; let it suffice if I tell you that the pol-filter is made of two slivers of glass which slide around one on top of the other. How far you cut down or eliminate reflections

21

depends on the angle between the reflecting surface and the source of the reflection, i.e. the sun or other light-source. You slide the glass slivers around until the reflection goes away. Pol-filters can also be used for black-and-white.

The sun-shield

This is an extra which is always invaluable, but never more than when taking colour-pictures. It keeps light-scatter away from the lens, and with side-light or light against you guards your lens from undesirable intrusion of light. It is a useful protection against splashing on the beach or when afloat. If you trip while carrying your camera, it will help protect your expensive lens from possible damage. All lenses require a specially fitted shield which is wide enough to cover the whole angle of vision.

Remember too that, if you are taking photos in the open air and wearing sun-glasses to cut down ultra-violet light, the slides you make are likely to be more than a little disappointing.

Clarity must be carried through to the background

There is no universal agreement as to the desirability of keeping the picture sharp all the way through from foreground to background. My own opinion is that in colour-pictures you need to have clarity all the way through, but this is not a hard rule. If you are taking a landscape scene, there is no hard objection to a certain fuzziness about the flowers right up in the foreground if that helps define more clearly one or two of the bits that are essential to your composition. Of course, there are also some subjects where it may be of the essence to blur the background a little, e.g. if you are taking a close-up in the open air. It may still be vitally important to have some object in the foreground which helps to make the main subject of the composition absolutely sharp, at the expense of blurring the middle and background. For that purpose you would need to use either a much bigger shutter-stopping or a lens with deeper focal length.

The attraction of the unusual

If you leaf through pictorial calendars, you will see normally only pictures that were taken in glorious sunshine. This will be even more likely with travel brochures. They have to influence potential customers. But in actual fact the sky is not always blue, the leaves are not evergreen, and the sea is highly changeable in colour. Do not just stow your camera away until the sun comes blazing out, but be on the look-out for subjects the other people will not be taking, i.e. unusual atmosphere, rare and exceptional compositions. There are, I hardly need say, marvellous pictures to be had just after a shower, once the clouds have passed away and the sunlight is sparkling in every little puddle.

Camera enemy No. 1

A wellknown successful photographer once said, "The motor-car is camera enemy number one". And very right too! You will only learn how to use your eyes properly if you go about on foot. This is a truism which will not seem very useful advice to all those whose feet have merely become parts of their car's clutch and accelerator. But it is the only road to the making of good colour-pictures. Running around in cars has ruined some people's faculty for looking at things quietly and taking them in. It has deprived them of vital areas of receptivity, even if these are not really vital faculties. You will not, the chances are, turn up unusual subjects on busy motorways, but off the beaten track along quiet footpaths is another matter. Moreover, you need, in addition to the ability to use your eyes and the ability to discriminate, a thorough mastery of the technical wrinkles. For really first-rate results, you need to be able to manage your camera with your eyes closed!

Always take more than one picture of your subject

Top professional photographers working in the open air always take at least two pictures, and sometimes even three or four, of any one subject, all at different exposures. Do not be too proud to follow their example, especially if it is a subject you will never get another chance of taking, either because the venue is too distant or because it is unlikely to happen again. Take one with the settings you obtain from your exposure meter, one with a slightly narrower opening and the third with a wider one. This is worth doing even if the subject is likely to be available a second time. It comes cheaper in the long run than having to revisit the subject all over again, and maybe waste your valuable time over it.

Treat it gently!

Colour-film is sensitive, and not only as regards exposure. Black-and-white is by its very nature more robust. Do not put colour-film into the car glove compartment, where it is likely to experience temperatures rising to 60 and 70ºC. The optimum temperature for keeping colour-film in good condition is around 12ºC. You will not always be able to be as careful as all that, but it is advisable to try. The film does not like the humidity to rise over 50% and high humidity is dangerous to it. If you meet such humidity levels accompanied by intense heat, you may well find that you cannot wind the film, or even load it for a start. I learned the truth of this to my cost on Tenerife. In hot countries it is a good idea to wrap unused film, still in its box, in silver paper and keep it in the fridge. Then 'break it in' gently to the temperature before you use it.

The first two sections having been given over to basic theoretical observations on the colour-film medium and the things needed to use it, this third section is an attempt to go into detail about suitable subjects for photography, with detailed treatment instructions. It has been considered easier for reference purposes to choose an alphabetical order of presentation. This permits the amateur to refer rapidly to what he wants.

AN ALPHABET OF SUBJECTS
AND HOW TO DEAL WITH THEM

Aerial photographs

People who fly are always tempted to have a shot at making aerial photographs, though the result is usually a let-down. To consider just one thing, the glass on the cabin-windows is never as clean as it ought to be for you to take a good shot, despite the fact that it is wiped over several times a day. Secondly, you are often using a lens which has too deep a focal length, and this makes you terribly susceptible to the dangers of wobbling. The most promising technique is to carry on with your normal lens and mask it with the Skylight filter. The best place to be is either right up front or at the back of the cabin. Whilst you are making your picture keep the lens as near to the window as possible. Breathe quite normally, but hold your breath whilst you are actually taking the picture. It is useful to exploit side-light or counter-light coming from one side. The most favourable weather condition is an absence of haze. Exposure-time at shutter-stop 5.6 = 1/250th or 1/500th sec., depending on the amount of contrast you want. Remember that there are legal restrictions on the publication of aerial photographs.

Animals (pictures on page 68)

I have included a special section on *PETS*. If you are set on stalking game in the woods, you had best seek advice from a proper forester first, who can tell you all about the animal's habits and movements. You will not achieve anything unless you prepare yourself. Before you go out looking for game, you should at least have cut your photographic teeth, so to speak, on pets and on animals in zoos. You will get a chance to practise in your garden if you set up a bird-table in winter. Either use a long-range lens or set the camera up beforehand close to the bird-table and connect the trigger and the flash to your window. If you know somebody professionally connected with animals he may give you the change to take photos in his cages. (Cf. *ZOOS* on page 70). If you are taking shots of fledglings in their nests, be careful not to upset them by making too much noise; you can even make life dangerous for them by cutting or bending branches nearby.

Aquaria (picture on page 28)

You cannot take photos of the denizens of aquaria without a flash; the natural light there is totally inadequate for photography. For one thing the fish often move very fast; for another, you need to stop down terrifically in order to reach the definition and depth you need. You will not achieve any worthwhile results unless you can set your camera up very close, either by using a magnifying lens, an extension ring or a scissors extension. It helps to equip the aquarium properly before you set to work, with a glass partition running the length of the tanks; this stops the fish swimming out of sight and keeps them all within the same plane. Set your camera up on a tripod straight in front of the front window of the tank. Never use a flash frontally, but let it off forward of the camera and held up either to right or left of it, so as to avoid the reflection of the flash in the window. It is a help if you can get a source of light from above, shining straight down inside the aquarium. If you can employ something of that sort, make sure it is to one side of your camera, with the light it gives off shining against the main lighting. It is as well to weaken the glare by covering this light with gauze or silk-screening. If you really want sharp pictures, you must have the front tank-window absolutely clean, and free of scratches or warping. If the fish are restless and sending up all kinds of floating distractions, wait patiently until these latter, which will only look unsightly in your picture, have settled. It is advisable to use daylight film. Mask your lens with the Skylight filter. Should you be the possessor of a long-focus lens, say 90mm., you will be lucky enough to be able to set your camera up a bit further off, and this should allow you to use the lighting to better advantage. (Cf. *CLOSE-UP* on page 31).

Architecture (pictures on pages 29 amd 33)

This is one of the most difficult subjects but one that is very much in favour, especially with tourists in Mediterranean countries. In narrow streets you will not achieve anything unless you use a wide-angle lens of 35 or even 28mm. focal length. But, when you use such lenses, watch out for the danger of getting distant lines seriously out of perspective. If you are lucky enough, you may be able to set to work from an elevated firing-position. This is particularly desirable if you want to take tall buildings, towers, etc. If the occupiers do not object, it is a good thing to take your photographs from neighbouring houses. It is much easier if you are in a situation to obtain a firing-position further off, than to use your normal lens and photograph normally from where you are. Lighting is the real clue. Partial side-lighting is the most advantageous of conditions because it emphasises the structure of brickwork and gives roundness to objects. Whatever you do, do not take photographs when the sun is very high or you will get over-strong shadows. Diffused lighting can sometimes be an advantage. A good many historic buildings are flood-lit at night; use daylight film by all means, as it gives warmer colouration. Always use the tripod where you can; it is next to impossible to keep quite still whilst holding the camera for as long as one or two seconds. Do not forget to train the exposure-meter on the bright bits of the subject when using reversal-colour film and on the dark bits when using negative.

Beaches

The first rule is to protect your lens from drifting sand. Go as close as you can to the subject whilst taking your picture, especially if the beach is crowded with bright bathing costumes. You do not want a multitude of colour-blobs. Playing children are photogenic, naturally, but adults put on airs and are best snapped by surprise - when they are going into the water, ploughing through the waves while swimming, splashing one another, playing games, or snoozing on their towels, or maybe, even making sand-castles; there is no shortage of promising subjects. Do not worry about counter-lighting - sea and sand will give you all the definition you will be wanting in your shadows. I know only one exception: the volcanic sand on almost all the Tenerife beaches is black. When taking photographs on beaches there, you should always use a light-shield; it is also wise to put on a Skylight filter or a polarisation filter as well. Do try out the Pol-filter and see how it alters and contrasts the colours of sky and water. You are hereby solemnly warned not to take photographs round midday. Beach-scenes are much above the average in brightness anyway; so narrow the shutter-stop from half to one whole value above what the exposure-meter gives you: go up from 8 to somewhere between 8 and 11 or go up even as much as 11.

Children (pictures on pages 41, 44 and 45)

Do let children play by themselves and do not strain to turn them into imitation adults, when you are taking their photographs. **3** or **4** months is when a baby starts reaching out to snatch at things. Try to shoot pictures of those first groping efforts! It would be wrong to shoot from the bird's eye vantage-point, down into the cot. Get down to the baby's level with your camera. Slightly diffused daylight is the best lighting. It is simple enough to brighten up the shadowy side with a white sheet or, even better, to use a screen made of gold foil; only be careful not to include either of these props in your picture. It is best to use a **90** to **135**mm. focal-depth lens and concentrate on getting the eyes sharp. You really cannot do without a long-range lens when the child gets older and is wide awake to what you are doing. Try to avoid posing techniques. The child playing on a lawn, in and near the water on its holidays gives you a plethora of chances, more than enough to enable you to dispense with having to fuss around with it. Let simplicity be your first commandment. This is not all that difficult to get, especially if you have a female assistant to distract the child's attention. You will have to use a flashlight indoors. There are first-rate pictures to be had in the bathroom during his (or her) bath. Bathroom walls, being light, will reflect the flash very strongly. Blue or red tiles may give you the sort of reflections you do not want. So it may well be best to direct the flash at the white ceiling or the sloping roof, if that is the kind of bathroom it is. Never flash frontally, so set off the flash forward of the camera and hold it up some way to one side, if you have to use the flash direct.

Churches

Church interiors can be most rewarding in colour, but they do demand considerable experience. It is essential to make the most of any lighting-contrasts. You will frequently see bright light falling through the elevated windows, many of them stained-glass. Unfortunately, by the time this light falls to ground-level it has all been swallowed up by the general dim religious light. If you take your measurements from the brightly-lit walls and pillars you will have pitch-dark shadows. If you take them from the fairly reasonable light in the nave, you will not obtain satisfactory versions of either the light subjects or the darker bits of the building. It is a useful improvisation to set your tripod up and use a narrow opening, set your stop on B and hold it there for as long an exposure as you require, while an assistant uncovers the dark bits of the nave for you by letting off an electronic or a blue bulb-flash. Your assistant can easily get out of the firing-line behind a projecting wall, in a niche, or behind a pillar. In any case do not do anything serious until you have carried out a dry run. Even then you may get let down. It is simpler to take pictures of separate details and isolated statues. Pictures of church exteriors present no inherent difficulties that have not already been referred to.

Close-up (pictures on pages 36 and 40)

How often do you hear people moaning bleakly, "I'd love to do close-ups but I can't ever get my camera any nearer than three feet (a meter)". This complaint is only partly justified. Most cameras, even the simplest models, have lenses which can be screwed on over the normal one or other close-up attachments. Screw-on close-up lenses require stopping down to 8 or 11, but that is something you would very likely do anyway, just to ensure getting the definition you wanted in the depths of the picture. There is one great advantage: attachments enable you to avoid spinning out your exposure-time. Using a suitable screw-on lens you can, if you are extremely lucky, get a result to the scale of one to three, which means you would capture an insect or a flower at a third of its proper size. Yet there is one considerable disadvantage. If you use a screw-on lens, do not trust the dimensions the viewfinder gives you. This is no handicap if you are using a reflex camera, or if you have a built-in exposure-meter or a telescopic sight. Distortion is worst in the case of small-picture cameras which have the viewfinder at the top of one side, because in that set-up both horizontal and vertical images require to be adjusted an half inch or so (20mm.). Some cameras do have anastigmatic correctors for this distortion, employing special close-up attachments. When working with screw-on lenses, you will do best to take a tape-measure and find out to the nearest half inch (10mm.) the distance between lens and subject.

There are also attachable range-finders which are specially designed for close-up work above or for both normal working and close ranges. I could list a host of suitable subjects; flowers, buds, tiny animals like birds, butterflies, beetles, etc. Many amateurs have had excellent results using a grey filter. This is something Kodak makes and you hold it up just in front of the subject, with the front turned half to the sun and half to the camera. You then measure the filter from a distance of 4-8 inches (100-200mm.) on your exposure-meter. When you are dealing with plants or animals in the open air, it is still necessary in most cases to use a flash (electronic or bulb).

Most commercial close-up attachments give you measurement-tables and working instructions, and these guarantee excellent results if you follow them properly. Here is one example:

Screw-on lenses for the 50mm standard lens

Screw-on lens	Stop	Distance in/cm	Reduction scale	Size of field of vision in/cm
f=100 cm (1 diopter)	∞	40/100	1:19	17.6x26.8/44x67
	6	34.4/86	1:16	14.8x22.8/37x57
	3	30/75	1:14	12.8x19.6/32x49
	1.5	23.6/59	1:11	10x11.6/25x29
	1	19.6/49	1:9	8.4x12.4/21x31
f =50 cm (2 diopters)	∞	20.4/51	1:10	9.2x13.6/23x34
	6	18.8/47	1:9	8.4x12.8/21x32
	3	17.6/44	1:8	7.6x11.6/19x29
	1.5	15.2/38	1:7	6.4x10/16x25
	1	13.2/33	1:6	5.6x8.4/14x21

f=30 cm	∞	13.6/34	1:6.4	6x8.8/15x22
(3 diopters)	6	12.8/32	1:6	5.6x8.4/14x21
	3	12/30	1:5.7	5.2x8/13x20
	1.5	11.2/28	1:5	4.8x7.2/12x18
	1	10/25	1:4	4.4x6.4/11x16
f=20 cm	∞	8.4/21	1:3.9	3.6x5.6/9x14
(5 diopters)	6	8/20	1:3.8	3.4x5.2/8.5x13
	3	7.6/19	1:3.6	3.32x5.04/8.3x12.6
	1.5	7.2/18	1:3.4	3.2x4.8/8x12
	1	6.8/17	1:3.1	2.84x4.4/7.1x11
	0.9	6.68/16.7	1:3	2.76x4.2/6.9x10.5

Evening (Cf. *TWILIGHT AND NIGHT*)

Fireworks

These can be very pleasing on colour-film, but they do require the use of a tripod to be really effective. It is pointless simply to take one or two occasional snaps; what you want is the effect of a number of rockets all coming down simultaneously. If you use daylight reversal-colour film, it will make the coloured stars and comet-tails look a good deal warmer but, if you use artificial-light film, they will look much cooler. However, artificial-light film also emphasises much better the velvety darkness of the night-time sky. Colour-negative has the advantage of reacting positively to natural light, artificial light, flashlight and even to an oil-lamp. It does not have a specifically sensitised colour-temperature, like reversal-colour. Set your camera up on a tripod, stop down to 5.6 and put the stop on T or B. A particularly good idea is to use a long-distance lead to your trigger fitted with a braking screw so that you do not have to keep your finger pressed down for any length of time. Set your distance to infinity. It is also as well to use a silhouette as foreground; what sort of silhouette is immaterial, a roundabout, a house, a tree or, best of all, a stretch of water so that you can have the flashes mirrored in it.

Flowers (pictures on pages 36 and 37)

A flower-bed containing a great number of flowers of various colours may be a sight that pleases the eye but it is not a very rewarding subject from the photographers point of view, especially if you are making small prints. This does not prevent an immense bed of tulips or a field entirely covered with wild poppies from having a certain photographic charm. There are many times when a section is better than the whole scene. There are no particular difficulties in photographing man-size flowers, larkspur, wild mallow or sunflowers. In sunlight conditions, shutter 8 at 1/125th sec. will be adequate, without needing to employ further aids to strengthen the lighting. But close-ups are a different kettle of fish. The wind is not content to whisper sweet nothings; it makes the thin-stemmed taller flowers sway sufficiently to make certain of giving you fuzzy pictures, even if the motion is hard to follow. Can you do anything about it? Yes. Even though you may not always succeed perfectly. You can try driving a stick into the ground and clipping the flowers to it with washing-pegs, making sure that these fastening devices are not visible to the camera; then you could try making windscreens from cardboard. If you cover these screens with crushed gold foil, they will also serve as auxiliary lighting screens. But beware of using coloured cardboard because the reflections from these distort the colours of the flowers. There will be times when these devices will not be enough to keep the wind at bay, because close-ups, to be sharp, require very severe stopping-down and consequently a similar amount of extra lighting time. In extreme cases of this kind, your only resource will be to use a flash. Since, as already noted, the stopping-down has to be acute, you run no danger of getting double outlines, as a result of taking both day and flashlight images. There are delightful effects to be obtained by employing an oblique counter-light on a completely still day, notably with tulips, lilies and roses. It makes the colours glow excitingly and gives the petals of the buds illuminated fringes which are sheer enchantment. If you are photographing very tall bushes, e.g. acanthus, sunflowers and hollyhocks, it is best to keep the sky as your background. Shoot upwards obliquely. If you want to take a close-up which isolates one special flower completely from its environment, there is no special difficulty about it. The flash will see to it that, using a very narrow aperture, you will lose the background entirely in gloom. There are other times where you will not need this hint, because you are trying to get the whole environment of the flower in with it. In this case use two flashlights, one on the main subject, the other on its environment. But keep the second flash down in intensity (using gauze or cheesecloth maybe). It is adequate if you just give hints of the environment in your picture. You will, of course, always use your tripod for taking this sort of picture.

Garden (picture on page 41)

A garden is a lovesome thing! It gives you subjects the whole year round just outside your front door, and what subjects! The glittering icicles hanging from the guttering, ice-flowers on the windowpane, rime on bare bushes and grasses, the first green buds on the shrubs, silvery catkins on the willow, snowdrop and crocus, tulip and daffodil, then in summer the splendid array of flowers, in autumn the discoloured foliage and the plump, red-cheeked apples. The important thing about any coloured pictures made in the garden is not to collect a riotous free-for-all but to take samples of closely matching colours. Since we are on home ground, we have all the time in the world to prepare the pictures. Nothing is going to run away! It can be a good idea to persuade one of our family to perk up the scene, either using a watering-can or secateurs. However, beware of their dress; it is best that it should be overall neutral in tone, cream, beige or grey; otherwise it may throw the picture off key.

Group-portraits

Whenever people mention groups, you think of all the fiddling preparations you went through at school when group-pictures were taken - how all the kids were built up in military blocks in age-groups or sets, with the kids in the back rows perched dangerously on forms. There is still no better way of taking a school-photo or any given group of thirty or forty people. Posed groups of this sort are obviously a pain in the neck to photograph, but they doubtless have value as souvenirs. There is no golden rule as to how to take a huge group without people

looking 'posed'. It is much simpler if your group is no larger than eight or twelve; then you can make them do all kinds of things that look natural, even if it is only sitting down and taking part in a chat. Small groups can also be split up into even smaller parties, with each separate group given something different to do. It is best to take a group-portrait from a slightly elevated position, like a chair or a stepladder; there is no need to hang from the chandelier, as a celebrated photographer has recommended! Let me deal first with groups outside. Many gardens have a swimming-pool, or at least a paddling-pool. Just set off a couple of your people playing paper-boats on the pool; you could have the children playing with the boats and the grown-ups looking on. Or you can collect a little group round the swing or sitting at a garden table. The main thing is to make them all look relaxed and to take them at the proper psychological moment. This is much more difficult indoors, especially if people have not much elbow-room in a small space. I recommend a wide-angle lens of 35 mm focal length. You should make some of the people play cards or chess, with the others looking over the players' shoulders. It is not likely that the natural light will be adequate on its own without your assistance, so help it along by employing a flash aimed at the white ceiling. Widen up the shutter by one value at least, or even two. Mean distance divided by the actual distance will give you the stopping you need, and you will do well to go up a notch or two, though you should not have to do that if you use a flash direct. Be very careful not to stagger your group too deeply, or the front-row faces will be as white as chalk and those in the rear as black as coal. You will not go wrong if you use the normal artificial lighting there is in the room whilst you are measuring up the group, but be certain to turn it off whilst actually taking the photograph, for reversal-colour does not take kindly to mixed lighting, though colour-negative does. It is possible to use ordinary household lights (preferably a fair number of them) if you are using artificial-light film or, and this is even better, photographic floodlights which will give you all the brightness you are likely to need. Do not forget one thing, whether indoors or out, and that is, to make sure you keep your background quiet. Bushes and ornamental plants are a distraction. (Cf. *PORTRAITS* on page 55).

42

Ice-flowers

It is not often you will be lucky enough to take ice-flowers against a red morning or evening sky. Nonetheless, you can help things forward by laying down some red silkscreen paper or, what is even better, putting a red gelatine foil screen in front of your flash. Set your camera up as for a close-up, with your lens getting to within at least 8 inches (200mm) from the subject. Do take a couple of test-shots first at a variety of different stoppings.

Interiors

There are three good ways of setting about interiors; either just use the light that comes in through the windows, fire a flash or use the normal artificial light. You are not likely to get the first opportunity very often, because all the light usually falls from one side of the room and as a consequence the opposite side of the room is lost in dark shadows. This is too stark a contrast for reversal-colour; even colour-negative does not react to it all that favourably. So give yourself a boost by exploiting some auxiliary source of lighting. Let us deal first with the camera: your most promising course is to employ a wide-angle lens that takes in most of the room and makes it look bigger without distorting it from the perspective angle. If the room is 8 feet (2.50m.) high, use the camera at a height of 4 feet (1.25m.) above the floor, and in a corner of the room. You will, of course, be using a firm tripod. Do not tilt the camera, or your lines will all come out slanting. If you employ a flash you need at least two bulbs, in order to project into even the most distant corners. When you use reversal-colour under artificial-light conditions, and, of course, when you use colour-negative too, there is nothing against employing normal photo floods in addition to the household lights you have already put on. Making the atmosphere of an interior really come to life is one of the photographer's toughest assignments. You will certainly have to try a number of test-shots first.

Landscapes (pictures on pages 21, 29, 48 and 73)

This is a very rewarding area and an inexhaustible one into the bargain. Only, do not try copying the average picture-postcard. Notwithstanding this warning, if it is an unfamiliar area you are

working in, postcards may be able to give you pointers to possible subjects. It is up to us to find views that have not been photographed before. Do not be shy of being choosy. This means looking through your viewfinder again and again, trying out new sections of the view, and new angles, not only if you use your normal lens, but with a long-range lens as well. What you want to take as a picture will be altering all the time. One great help may be the so-called vario-lens with adjustable focal length, which is not unlike the film-camera zoom-lens. Once you are sharply onto a subject, you may alter the focal length as much as you like without needing to get your picture re-focused all over again. The so-called macro-zoom-lens will cover all subjects from infinity to 1:2. That really is what may be called a boon! But I must not hide the fact that the optical quality is not the same at all focal lengths. There are bound to be some fractional distortions. Sometimes one detail will say more about a landscape than a vast panorama of the whole thing which tries to squeeze it all together into one lump. It is always a help to have a warm-toned foreground of yellow, orange or red. If that is not possible, bump the foreground up a bit by patting in, artlessly, yellow or red flowers. These will be a help even if they do come out slightly fuzzy. It is also not impossible to get down to worm's eye level and incorporate wild flowers into the picture in their natural place. The best times for photography are early morning and very late afternoon, though you will have to exercise a good deal of discretion about this in the darker seasons of the year. After a big change in the weather, as well as after a thunder-storm, you will see magnificent piles of clouds and exciting lighting effects. If you want a sky with lots of clouds, give it two-thirds of the print; if you want to emphasise what is at ground-level, proceed the other way round. In black-and-white photography, it is useful to have a line, i.e. for this purpose a road, a stream or fence, leading straight into the picture. In colour-photography, the same effect may be obtained by exploiting a strip of colour. Be wary about putting too much green into the picture. For this reason a good time to go to work is spring, when the green patches are still light in tone and strongly contrasting, or else in autumn or winter. If you should happen to strike brilliantly contrasting lighting, train your exposure-meter on the bright bits and give up any idea of getting detail in the darker areas. You should measure up for the dark bits, of course, if you are using colour-negative. You will get stronger colours if you use a polarisation filter.

Macro-pictures (pictures on pages 52 and 53)

They give you the subject much larger than it is under normal conditions. The macro area starts at the scale of 1:1 and finishes up when you go for a micro-photograph. Macro-photography has come increasingly into favour of recent years, and rightly so, because it allows us to perceive things which are otherwise hidden away. To take proper macro-pictures you require a reflex camera with extending attachment or telescopic lens, or a reflex camera with built-in exposure-meter, extending attachment or telescopic lens. The shorter the focal length, the bigger you can make your subject turn out. It is essential to site the lens as close as possible to the subject. If you employ the magnificent magnifying lens in order to get the picture to the small scale you want, you will have to get to within millimeters of your subject; this is not likely to come off with living creatures that are at all shy. With these the employment of flash-bulbs also presents difficulties. If you are dealing with subjects that keep perfectly still, you may be able to do entirely without flashing, particularly if you can build up the lighting to your own satisfaction with the help of sunlight and mirrors, and do not stop down too much. Light decreases in intensity at the rate of the quadruple of the distance. If you use extending attachments or a telescopic lens you will have to stand quite a long way from the plane against which you have the subject posed. These are the exposure-tables:

Increased distance away from subject	1½ times focal length	Double exposure-time
Increased distance away from subject	twice focal length	Quadruple exposure-time
Increased distance away from subject	three times focal length	Nine times exposure-time

If you want your picture to be on the scale of 1:1, you will require no less than four times normal exposure-time. This is where you start running into difficulties as to the size your prints will turn out, let alone what is going to happen if you want to work to any larger scale. Since it is almost impossible under normal conditions to obtain exposure-times of this order, you are left with the expedient of using the electronic or the bulb-flash. If you are in a tight corner, you could always try a micro-copying lamp or even a slide projector. You can focus the light effectively by fencing in the nozzle with a paper tube. A small screen made of gold foil will brighten up the shadowy side. Another possible aid is the auxiliary flash-bulb. Whether in any given situation you use half-strength flash-lighting or soften down the normal light from your lamp depends to a large extent on the chiaroscuro effect your subject already has. No amount of theoretical lecturing is as useful as experiencing the process yourself, especially if you go about things in a thorough, paced, scientific fashion. You will obtain the best and most consistent results if you start with a series of dry runs, noting down your figures scrupulously so that you can go back to the old values whenever you so desire. There is also a very easily mastered lightning ready-reckoner you can buy at no very great cost; it has a revolving calculating-disc and fits easily into the pocket.

Mountains

The majesty and sublimity of mountainscapes are almost irresistible. So you will not be surprised if I am insistent on the circumspection with which you ought to use your camera in the mountains. When you are on a mountain-trek, every extra pound you take with you becomes an additional encumbrance, so be sparing in choosing what photographic equipment you intend to have with you. Unless you are going to set out deliberately to photograph mighty panoramas, you can happily jettison your wide-angle lens. All the same, you really need to give your normal lens a focal length of 90 or 135mm. The first basic rule is: never take pictures with the light behind you, but always have it coming from the side or as a side counter-light. Get up early and sample the early morning atmosphere, when the mist is lying in the valleys. The second one is this: you must have a good foreground; it may be only a footpath leading diagonally into the picture, a sagging fence, a wayside shrine, a jagged comb of rock or a young fir. Useful foregrounds in colour-pictures are rhododendrons or arnica in full bloom. The polarisation filter is an excellent servant in the mountains in the way it effectively throttles blue interference and enhances the luminescence of the colours; it also brings definition into misty distances. There is no agreement as to the advisability or not of using the UV filter at heights over 5000 feet (1500 metres). Modern high-definition lenses do not really need it, being made in such a way as to cut ultra-violet light anyway. (Cf. the entry *WINTER*).

Night-photography (pictures on pages 56 and 57)

Is it possible to photograph in the night-time? It is indeed, and not only after a heavy fall of snow or in bright moonlight. In town, too, you can obtain magnificent effects in misty drizzle and after showers, when the street-lights are reflected in the washed asphalt, and everything is surrounded by a halo of light. If that is the effect you want, you will have to spend some of your time making test pictures to study first, so as to find out the best exposure-times which you can use again and again whenever you want something of the same kind.

Lively street-scenes when the lights are on, at twilight, should only be photographed with daylight films, or colour-negative film, though the out-side lighting may be dodgy. Daylight film makes the colours of the lights much warmer. If, contrariwise, what you are after are the blue shadows of the twilight and the special effects they make, use artificial-light film. Unfortunately, it so happens that nowadays the streets are being lit, not only by normal electric-light bulbs, but also by ionised light, strip-lighting which is warm and white in tone, and by halogen and mercury-vapour lights; these lights all have diverging colour-temperatures. When you add the immense number of different sorts of illumination used in window-dressing you realise the dilemma you are in when it comes to making up your mind between daylight and artificial-light film. You can even take successful snapshots if you use a wide-open stop and very sensitive colour-film; if you want something more than a quick shot, it is much better to use your tripod. Exposures of more than two minutes are liable to be

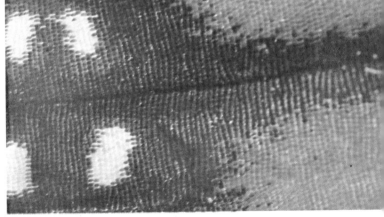

affected by the Schwarzschild Effect (under-exposure, colour-interference), so it is advisable to stick to the instructions leaflet. To work out the advantages and disadvantages of the two types of colour-film, try out one roll of artificial-light film and one roll of daylight-film and make a series of five or six exposures at different stoppings, keeping the other data equal.

Exposure-times for night-photography

	Reversal-colour 18 DIN/50 ASA artificial-light film
Christmas tree with, maybe, 20 candles without auxiliary lighting	1-2 secs. Stop 4
With other interior lighting and people standing by the tree	½-1 sec. Stop 4
	Reversal-colour 18 DIN/50 ASA daylight film
Streets with Christmas illuminations	1/4-1/8th sec. Stop 2.8 - 4
Floodlit building	1-3 secs. Stop 4
Brightly lit shop-windows	1/10th-1/5th sec. Stop 2 - 4
Fireworks	B or T 1-3 secs. Stop 5.6 - 11

Pets

It is not as easy as you might think to get a good picture of one of our four-legged friends. People tend to photograph them 'from a great height', i.e. from the human standpoint, which gets things all wrong. If you want to photograph a dog, a rabbit or a cat, it is better to put yourself on their level. Use as neutral a background as you can - if the animal is light in colour, use a dark background, and vice versa. If you are in open country or in the garden, do not let obtrusive objects, bushes etc. clutter the background. As a background, sky goes almost dead-white, because reversal-colour is not up to the enormous contrast between very pale blue and, say, the sandy colour of a wire-haired dachshund. The boot is on the other foot where we are faced with a white or sandy-furred cat. You can take photographs of really big animals from shoulder-height without affecting the result adversely. When you are trying to take animals, even pets, the flash-gun can be an asset. You will need the flash in order to get detail into the fur, to lighten up shadows and tone down movement. Provided that the animals do not worry at being watched, you can obtain excellent results with a 90-105mm. lens or even a 135mm. focal length. The things you particularly need to have right are the eyes; pay special attention to the iris and its light-point. Your pictures will look very sad if the animals are drooping about all over them, obviously at a loose end for something to do, and showing signs of being off-colour. Take dogs for example: you should play with them for a while first and let them wear themselves out until they hang out their tongues and generally look avid for fresh air. A few subjects to be specially recommended are such as: a cock crowing, a kitten playing with a ball of wool, or lapping milk from a bowl.

Portraits (pictures on pages 56 and 57)

Indoors or outside. That is the question. When the amateur goes into the 'Great Out-Doors', he normally 'shoots' his 'victims' from a distance of 10-20 feet (4-6m.), which makes the faces much too tiny. Moreover there is a tendency to cram into the picture, all sorts of things which only serve to distract. Using the normal lens of a small-picture camera, which has a 50mm. focal length, you may safely get up to within 5 feet (1.5m.) of your

'victim'. 90mm. and 135mm. attachable lenses are a great help too. This means you can stay further off and make the subject less self-conscious; it also means you get more of their face. No one is forcing you to cram in all of his or her neck and shoulders. The long-focus lens has one more extra advantage; it makes the background even fuzzier. Out of doors the best background is simply, at all times, the sky; failing that a neutral-toned wall not too close to the subject. Watch out for intrusive trees and shrubs! Bright sunshine is not the best of conditions for the taking of a good portrait out of doors; it gives you dark shadows round the eyes and nose and makes the sitter screw up his or her eyes. Much more favourable conditions are those when there is light and fluffy cloud-cover blotting out the sun at frequent intervals. Colour-portraits should not be taken amongst trees, since the reflections from the leaves turn faces green. Red garden-umbrellas turn pallid faces red. It is advisable to take aim with your exposure-meter right up to 8 inches (200m.) from the sitter's face. It is not enough simply to say, "Smile and say cheese!" The artful photographer can soften his 'victim' by distracting him with witty chatter.

Since you will have your shutter wide open, you can depend on getting a sudden snap, catching the momentary expression which pleases you best. Girls and women are often most flatteringly photographed in profile. The reflection of the lighted edging round hair, forehead, nose and chin makes the face more interesting. It does not matter if the rest of the face looks slightly under-exposed. The thing you do not want under any circumstances is full frontal lighting. It makes faces flat and squeezes out the features. Diffused light, as stated previously, is the thing you really need, such as we have when the sun is ever so slightly overcast. Another tip: all your sitters will have one 'nice' profile. Watch out for it when you take a portrait. The less colour your picture has, the happier you will be. Taking portrait photos indoors: this is dodgy; for few amateurs have a proper studio set-up which allows them to employ a battery of floods and create their own diffused light. If the room takes in diffused daylight, it ought to be possible to take the portrait near the window, and this will allow you to stop down as much as you like. But do watch out to see that the greenery outside is not sending coloured light into the room. Use your exposure-meter on that profile which is turned to the light. Electronic or blue-bulb flashlight is much akin to natural light. The most advantageous thing you can bring to bear is a battery of two flash-guns, so that you can employ one of them as your main lighting, a little to one side and slightly higher than the camera, while you use the second one a little further away in order to brighten up the shady side. Watch out not to get shadows on both sides of the nose; to avoid this it is a good idea to dim down the second gun by covering it with a screen of thin material. Another possible way of using your battery would be to use one gun as your main source of light not quite vertically over the camera, and the second to give you reflection from the ceiling (which has to be a white one!) Using reversal-colour under artificial-light conditions, you may require help from all the household lamps you can lay your hands on, or, better still, some 250-1000 watt photo-floods. In any case you ought to be using a couple of floods. Even if you **are** using some it is still possible to use white flash-bulbs. Particularly exciting portraits can be taken using an ordinary 100 watt table-lamp, with the sitter directly under the lamp, reading maybe. It is a useful hint to catch the sitter in profile, so that the half of their face which is turned away from the light is lost in shadow.

Snapshots (pictures on pages 27 and 39)

There are times when you need to be very quick off the mark, e.g. in markets, on a dockside, in a children's playground or on the sports field. Even if you use your trigger without shaking the camera, you will only obtain a successful print if you get the exposure-time right. The following are the figures for reversal-colour, daylight, 18 DIN/50 ASA:

Snapshot settings for 50mm. and 75mm. focal length

setting	Stop	gives you definition
13 feet/4m.	8	9.5 to 23 feet/3m. to 7m.
32 feet/10m.	8	16 feet to ∞/5m. to ∞

Good light is a pre-requisite, but not necessarily sunshine. For things moving fast you need your shutter wider open, and this will cut down your definition in depth. Even when the weather is dull, you really ought to widen your shutter one value. If you are having to photograph from very close to, say up to 9.5 feet (3m.), it will be mandatory to stick very close to what the exposure-meter gives you. If you are using a reflex camera, one with a built-in exposure-meter or an automatic camera, aiming and setting are so simple and quick that you do not really need any special drill for snaps; but I will still give you the basics. If the lighting is exceptionally favourable, you will be able to stop down as far as 11, and this will greatly improve your definition in depth. Following this line up to 13 feet/4m, shutter 11, f = 2.60; up to 26 feet/8m, shutter ditto, f = 6 distances from 14 feet/4.3m. to infinity.

Sport (picture on page 68)

When taking pictures at sporting events, you can follow for most purposes what was said about *SNAPSHOTS*, but there are some things which need to be stated as well. Do not photograph sprinters or jumpers from the side, but from the front or at a sharp angle. Take aim at a fixed point on the track or above the bar, and fire at the crucial instant. When dealing with high jumpers, pole vaulters or show jumpers, there is one short second of dead calm, as they attain the very top of their parabola: exploit it! Crouching is the easiest position to take photographs from. In order to get the shortest exposures, you will need the shutter as wide open as possible. Remember it is only the actual subject that has to be sharp. There are tables giving you the most favourable exposure-times; their value is debatable, because there are so many variables involved - lighting, distance away, angle to the movement of the subject (are you going to be straight on or slightly on the skew?), focal length of the subject, etc., etc. The sensitivity of the film also plays a part, naturally. To give you something to go on, let me just mention a few figures, though I should also stress that they are all for events that are taking place at right angles to the camera:

distance of subject =				
	16 ft/5m	40 ft/12m	82 ft/25m	164 ft/50m
Runners	1/500th	1/500th	1/250th	1/125th
Cyclists	1/250th	1/250th	1/125th	1/60th
Horse trotting	1/500th	1/250th	1/125th	1/60th
Horse cantering	1/1000th	1/500th	1/250th	1/125th
Racing cars	1/1000th	1/1000th	1/500th	1/250th

Sun

No matter how little experience they have, you will not find any amateur who is such a lunatic as to take a photograph straight into the blazing sun; he knows that he will not get anything for dazzle. On the other hand, it is not wholly unusual to find yourself in the kind of sunlight where you can look into the sun without blinking, and this you can include in your picture. Such opportunities you find mainly in the early morning and late in the evening. The inexperienced photographer usually over-exposes on these occasions, because he is worrying too much about the side which is turned away from the sun. If, for example, you are taking pictures of the sun setting by a lake, it would be wrong to train your exposure-meter on the reeds standing in the foreground. The result after all that would be a gutless and colourless, washed-out sky. Do not bother about turning the foreground into a simple silhouette. Aim your exposure-meter at the sky and hang the consequences! That will enhance the brilliance of the sunset yellow, orange and red. At moments such as these you really cannot do without the sun-shield. Do not be mean with your footage if the spectrum of colours is changing all the time. There is not a great deal of profit to be made out of sunsets when the middle-ground is full of greens; they go an unpleasant colour under the influence of all that red. If the sun is only a tiny glowing sphere in the sky, the normal lens will bring it in as only a very tiny object; this is a good reason for using a deeper focal length, say 200mm. plus.

Travel (picture on page 73)

Let me kick off by giving you four absolute rules for holiday travel:

1 Keep your camera clean and make sure that everything is in working order.

2 If you are using anything that needs batteries, change them every so often or take reserve batteries along with you.

3 Check your flash-gun or your electronic flash, charge up your flashing equipment, top the condenser up with distilled water, if it needs it, change the battery in the flash-gun.

4 Do not forget to take the parts for your flashes with you.

Get a supply of colour-film in store, because it is frequently more expensive and not always fresh if you buy it abroad. If you are going in your car, be careful not to put the spare film in your glove-compartment because this can turn into a baking-oven. It is best of all to carry the film in a refrigerated hold-all, especially if it is the Mediterranean for which you are heading. Put an air-drier (silicagel) in with the films, and that will deal with any occasional humidity. If you keep your colour-film in a refrigerator while you are on holiday, remember to give the film time to warm up to the climate after you have taken it out of the cold. Most people take photographs of historic buildings, ancient monuments and ornamental fountains, etc. I will not carp at that... But do not put your friends up in front of these structures. The kind of picture you get from that will never amount to anything more than a 'holiday souvenir'. It is always better to make the people do the things that are appropriate to the spot, e.g. have people in the foreground inspecting a building in the background. Monumental buildings are very likely to be way beyond the capacity of your size of print or come out so small that you will not be able to make out any significant details. Prints of isolated bits of detail frequently mean much more. Pictures taken with the long-range lens have a habit of distorting the perspective. Do not invariably take the same picture from the same spot thousands of other keen photographers have used before you. There is still a great deal waiting to be discovered and proclaimed. Put your colour-film, as soon as you have exposed it, straight back into its tin box and shut it up fast; it is best to cover the join where it opens with sticky tape, into the bargain. Get it developed as soon as is feasible.

Twilight (picture on page 32)

Lots of prints which are passed off as night-pictures were actually made in the twilight; but this is not sleight-of-hand. If you want to use your camera in the street, and the street is illuminated from all sorts of varying light-sources, you really ought to be employing daylight reversal-colour. It is, of course, entirely likely that you will suffer from slight yellow interference, but that sort of colour-scheme is much more acceptable than the artificial-light film, which makes the colours chillier. Which you finally settle for is entirely up to you. Let me now suggest a few rewarding subjects: a street with masses of shop-windows filled with coloured advertising lights and passing cars sweeping by with their dipped headlights and red tail-lights, all reflected on brightly-lit wet roads so that they leave a long trail behind them. Using ultra-sensitive 23 DIN reversal-colour, you may even bring off some successful snapshots on brightly-lit streets at shutter 2.8 or even 4. All bright subjects need is 1/8th - 1/25th sec. It is best to lean on a wall or something to give your arms steadying support. If what you are after are medium-bright or darker subjects it is better to use the tripod. (Cf. to the entries *NIGHT-PHOTOGRAPHY* and *SUN!)*

Waterfalls

Cascades tumbling and hissing down from mountains are favourite subjects for photographers. There is no problem in the kind of countryside where there are no trees or other obstacles to a clear line of sight. Let me advise you to steer clear of the waterfall that is surrounded by lots of shade-casting trees in the midst of thick woods; the print is bound to be a let-down, because you are likely to suffer shocking blue interference. The first pre-requisite for a good print of a waterfall is to have counter-light striking sparks off the water and brightening the general effect up no end. I shall not repeat here, in the usual tedious way, the often imparted advice not to under-expose falling water and surf. Do not stop down under 1/250th sec. or you will simply make the tossing waters look like porridge. Get as close as you can; it will not matter if the foreground looks slightly fuzzy.

Winter (picture on page 68)

Snow and ice reflect the blue of the sky like mirrors. Of course, what the eye sees normally are expanses of smooth, clear and spotless white. If you keep your eyes wide open, though, you will notice that round midday the snow is dappled by lots of obviously blue shadows. At sunrise and sunset, on the other hand, it goes a pronounced yellow and orange. Colour-film reproduces all these tints faithfully. The best time for photographing in the snow is actually right after a snowfall, even though it is unlikely you will enjoy as clear and sunny a sky at that sort of time as you might like, under ideal conditions. Get used to taking photographs with the aid of side-and counter-light, because these are the conditions which electrify the ice-crystals and make them give off myriads of tiny sparkling points of light. Be careful to choose a suitable and effective foreground, in colours which are as warm as they can be. It should not be difficult to get hold of a boy in a red or yellow jumper pulling a sledge after him, or a bush, e.g. a rowan with red berries. Do not turn your nose up at the less exciting subjects, like a branch of wild rose covered with rime. That sort of subject, too, needs side- and counter-lighting. If the light is dull, use your flash as a sun-substitute. Do not think it too much effort to go down to the frozen pond to watch the skaters. And do not be too much of a snob to go up with the skiers into the mountains. If you are having good sun and there is a respectable side-light, skiing slaloms and jumps are ideal fodder for the colour-camera: with 18 DIN/50 ASA and shutter 5.6., your exposure-times need be no more than 1/250th and 1/500th sec. Get one particular point completely in focus and then press your trigger as the people go by. Just a word about the exposure-meter which, when faced with limitless sweeps of flat snow, tends to go crazy. As a machine, the meter is built to cope with middling values, and tends to give exposures which are much too short to deal with all that blinding white. Always open your shutter one value further than the meter gives you here. You will not need that amount of adjustment if the subject has contrasty lighting, i.e. if there are big shafts of strong light and shade, or if

the light is all coming towards you; these conditions will light up the snow by themselves and do not need any assistance to set the snow-crystals twinkling. If you employ frontal light, your prints are likely to be wash-outs.

Work (pictures on pages 60 and 61)

Men at work! Not the most wildly popular of subjects, but it has all sorts of interesting potentialities. You will not find millions of artisans beaming to have their picture taken at their anvil, lathe or whatever; they usually prefer to doll themselves up a bit before-hand. So tread carefully; remember that what you are looking for is the representation of a living person - you are interested in his concentration - you want to show him looking into recognisable details of his work. Show then the whole human spectrum and take it as it comes; do not try to do too much fiddly stage-managing. That is not to say that a little scene-shifting never improves anything. Indoors you had best use the flash-gun, not frontally, if you can avoid it, but held away from the camera and about 45° to one side. You do want to get your main focus of interest on the worker and his inspired hands. If you do not want to get him altogether detached from his background, do not stop down too far; then his background will be as sharp as his face. You do not always have to take your photographs at arm or chest-level; it is quite an idea to photograph working activities from a crouch, especially if this makes what is going on turn out more understandable. All sorts of subjects come to mind: the tool-bench, machine-controls, all sorts of handicrafts and lots of farming and dockside work. You will not suffer from any lack of choice! The liveliest prints will probably be the ones you snapped in the open air. For these you must really work the distance out in advance and use a fairly deep focal-length lens.

Zoos (pictures on pages 68 and 69)

We all know the story of the maniac who goes rushing about the zoo, jumping from cage to cage and enclosure to enclosure, snapping everything he can catch passing in front of his shutter. His prints are pretty dreadful, because you must consider where you are when you are working in a zoo and what demands the unnatural conditions make on the camera. The lighting, the bars, the distances, how the animals are behaving, all these things are crucial. If you want to make good zoo pictures, you will need time, lots of time; you will also need patience and sticking-power. Watch your animal before you press your trigger. Each animal has a more or less typical stance; each has his own behavioural quirks; each is an individual, even if different species do have common types of activity. If the animals are easy to get near, you can safely use your normal lens. If they are in an open enclosure or separated from the public by moats or ditches, you will need a long-range attachment. This will enlarge the victim as much as you want, and ensure that distracting bits of his background turn out suitably fuzzy. I mentioned sticking-power before: the light will not always be right; you may get just the picturesque grouping you have been chasing, but it will be covered by great, thick bars of shadow: so give it up and come back later. As the sharpest point in your picture, go by the reflections you can see in the nearest open animal eye. If the animal's skin or fur is dark, stop up a half- or one whole value. Zoo authorities do not look with favour on flashes or flash-bulbs; most, if not all the animals are sensitive to sudden bursts of light. If the light in the zoo is excessively poor, you had better use reversal-colour in one of the 23 DIN/160 ASA varieties. Some of the most interesting pictures are there to be 'shot' at feeding times.

SLIDES AND HOW TO PROJECT THEM

Coloured photos (prints) ought really to be stored in a special album, to keep the light off them. If you want to have them hanging on the wall, cover them with protective varnish or the specially made plastic sheeting you can buy in camera shops. Coloured slides are also sensitive to a degree to light. You can ask the developing lab to mount them for you, only if you do they will make you pay for your unwanted results as well. So the best thing to do is to become your own mounter. But do exercise patience when the developed film comes back to you, and give it twenty-four hours to settle down and get rid of the last droplets of moisture. My advice is to build your own trial-viewer for the negative strips. All this needs is a 15-watt bulb and a sheet of milky glass. It is best to do this testing in a blacked-out room. Keep the negatives some distance away from the screen in order not to get the slide too hot. If you can obtain a magnifying lens which blows up the slide to six or eight times bigger than the original, you will spot all the mistakes and fuzzy bits as clearly as you want.

What sort of mount?

There is a wide choice. If you have lots of time on your hands, you can prepare the necessary bits of paper and make your own mounts and your own covers and your own glass protection. There are two main types of commercial frames available, the ones in which negatives can be changed, and fixed ones which they cannot. Some developing labs send you back your slides covered with a protective film which obviates the need for glass protection. Even if you want to have interchangeable pictures, you should keep them in dust-proof frames, not accepting any frame as 100% tight. Dust is your worst enemy; it is just waiting to settle on your negatives. So you have to fight it even before you start hiding your negatives away under glass. Wipe them over with anti-static cloth or a very fine brush. Then go over them with a magnifying glass. Make sure you do not wear a woollen sweater whilst working with the negatives; wool makes lots of fluff.

How to beat the Newton Ring Effect

If the shiny side of your slide negative is too close to the glass, or if the film has not properly dried out, you will get rainbow-coloured shapes running all over it. The best remedy for this is to let the film dry thoroughly and use de-Newtonised glass against the shiny side. Against the matt side you do not need anything other than plain glass. Even these precautions do not offer you 100% protection against the possibility that you will have Newton rings forming. When handling slides, be careful always to put the matt side, not the shiny side, facing the light-bulb. It ought to be adequate to mark the mount in coloured pencil or with sticky coloured tape. If necessary, it may also be a useful safeguard against projecting upside-down slides, to put a special mark in a top corner.

The projector

The numbers of projectors available are growing all the time. There are very simple machines with manual slide controls, half-automatic and fully automatic ones, and even some makes on which you control slide-changing and focussing from a distance. A simple set-up is all you need for family showings. If you aim higher, you will have to invest a great deal more. Projectors equipped with low-voltage and halogen bulbs have the advantage of keeping your slides from exposure to great blasts of hot air.

The screen

Buy a good screen. There is no inherent reason why you should not use a white wall or a sheet, but you will not get the luminescence you should in either case. Too much light is being swallowed up. Slides look their best if projected onto a crystal-pearl or silver-coated screen. Project straight at the screen, aiming the lens at the centre. There are cheap plastic screens in the shops, good, if you do not use them too often and too long.

Ring the changes!

Do not bore the audience with a monotonous show. People always do want to show too many slides at one go; this is a case where economy is a luxury. Whatever your basic theme is, ring the changes between total and less-than-total views, close-ups and macro-pictures. Do not put on a whole sequence of 6-7 slides full of green or blue, but break up the monotony with a few other slides in warmer colours. Always try your programme out first on your own family and a circle of friends who are not afraid of speaking their minds. Slides can easily be linked with a tape-recorder; nowadays there is apparatus available for synchronising what you see with what you hear.

Size of image (in/cm) using normal small slides

Projection distance in feet/metres	Focal Length			
	=85mm	=100mm	=120mm	=150mm
6.5/2	22.2x24/ 53x60	18.4x27.2/ 46x68	17.2x26/ 43x65	11.6x12.2/ 29x43
10/3	32x48/ 80x120	27.2x40.8/ 68x102	23.2x34.4/ 58x86	17.2x26/ 43x65
13/4	46.8x64/ 117x160	36x54,4/ 90x136	30.8x44.8/ 77x112	24.8x37.2/ 62x93
16.5/5	54x81.2/ 135x203	46x68.8/ 115x172	38.4x57.6/ 96x144	30.8x44.8/ 77x112
19.5/6	65.2x81.2/ 163x203	46x68.8/ 115x172	38.4x57.6/ 96x144	30.8x44.8/ 77x112
26/8	86.8x130/ 217x325	74x111.2/ 185x278	51.2x92/ 153x230	48.4x72.8/ 121x182

INDEX OF SUBJECTS CHOSEN FOR DISCUSSION